BULL'S-EYE

BULL'S-EYE

A PHOTOBIOGRAPHY OF ANNIE OAKLEY

BY SUE MACY

FOREWORD BY BESS EDWARDS

NATIONAL GEOGRAPHIC SOCIETY

WASHINGTON, D.C.

For Hannah, a pioneer girl at heart—SM

Staff for this book

Jennifer Emmett, *Project Editor*
Suzanne Patrick Fonda, *Editor*
Bea Jackson, *Art Director*
Marty Ittner, *Designer*
Callie Broaddus, *Associate Designer*
Jo H. Tunstall, *Assistant Editor*
Paige Towler, *Editorial Assistant*
Meredith C. Wilcox, *Illustrations Coordinator*
Carl Mehler, *Director of Maps*
XNR, *Map Research and Production*
Lewis R. Bassford, *Production Manager*
Bobby Barr, *Manager, Production Services*

Published by the National Geographic Society

Gary E. Knell, *President and CEO*
John M. Fahey, *Chairman of the Board*
Melina Gerosa Bellows, *Chief Education Officer*
Declan Moore, *Chief Media Officer*
Hector Sierra, *Senior Vice President and General Manager,
    Book Division*

Senior Management Team, Kids Publishing and Media

Nancy Laties Feresten, *Senior Vice President;* Jennifer
Emmett, *Vice President, Editorial Director, Kids Books;* Julie
Vosburgh Agnone, *Vice President, Editorial Operations;* Rachel
Buchholz, *Editor and Vice President,* NG Kids *magazine;*
Michelle Sullivan, *Vice President, Kids Digital;* Eva Absher-
Schantz, *Design Director;* Jay Sumner, *Photo Director;* Hannah
August, *Marketing Director;* R. Gary Colbert, *Production Director*

Digital

Anne McCormack, *Director;* Laura Goertzel, Sara Zeglin,
Producers; Jed Winer, *Special Projects Assistant;* Emma
Rigney, *Creative Producer;* Brian Ford, *Video Producer;* Bianca
Bowman, *Assistant Producer;* Natalie Jones, *Senior
Product Manager*

Copyright © 2001 Sue Macy; reprinted in paperback and library
binding, 2015
Published by the National Geographic Society.
All rights reserved. Reproduction of the whole or any part of the
contents without written permission from the publisher is prohibited.

The body text of the book is set in Minister light. The display text is
Latin condensed and Algerian condensed, and the quotes appear in
Caflisch Script.

The Library of Congress cataloged the 2001 edition as follows:
Macy, Sue.
    Bulls-eye : a photobiography of Annie Oakley / by Sue Macy.
    p. cm.
Includes index.
    ISBN 978-0-7922-7008-9
    1. Oakley, Annie, 1860-1926—Juvenile literature. 2. Shooters of
firearms—United States—Biography—Pictorial works—Juvenile
literature. 3. Entertainers—United States—Biography—Pictorial
works—Juvenile literature. [1. Oakley, Annie, 1860-1926. 2.
Sharpshooters. 3. Entertainers. 4. Women—Biography.] I. Title:
Photobiography of Annie Oakley. II. National Geographic Society (U.S.)
III. Title.
GV1157.03 M33 2001
799.3'092—dc21
2001000125

2015 paperback edition ISBN: 978-1-4263-2218-1
2015 Reinforced Library Binding ISBN: 978-1-4263-2232-7

The National Geographic Society is one
of the world's largest nonprofit scientific
and educational organizations. Founded
in 1888 to "increase and diffuse geographic
knowledge," the Society's mission is to
inspire people to care about the planet. It reaches more
than 400 million people worldwide each month through its
official journal, *National Geographic,* and other magazines;
National Geographic Channel; television documentaries;
music; radio; films; books; DVDs; maps; exhibitions; live
events; school publishing programs; interactive media; and
merchandise. National Geographic has funded more than
10,000 scientific research, conservation, and exploration
projects and supports an education program promoting
geographic literacy.

For more information, please visit nationalgeographic.com,
call 1-800-NGS LINE (647-5463), or write to the following
address:
National Geographic Society
1145 17th Street N.W.
Washington, D.C. 20036-4688 U.S.A.

Visit us online at nationalgeographic.com/books

For librarians and teachers: ngchildrensbooks.org

More for kids from National Geographic: kids.
nationalgeographic.com

For information about special discounts for bulk purchases,
please contact National Geographic Books Special Sales:
ngspecsales@ngs.org

For rights or permissions inquiries, please contact National
Geographic Books Subsidiary Rights:
ngbookrights@ngs.org

**Cover: In this early portrait, Annie wore one of
the many medals presented to her by admirers.**

**Title Page: Annie often shot apples off the head
of her dog, Dave. Wrote one reporter, "Dave
possesses a great deal more nerve than most of
his human brethren, for he never flinches."**

**Opposite: A publicity shot of Annie for Buffalo
Bill's Wild West show**

National Geographic supports K–12 educators with ELA
Common Core Resources. Visit natgeoed.org/commoncore
for more information.

Printed in China
14/RRDS/1

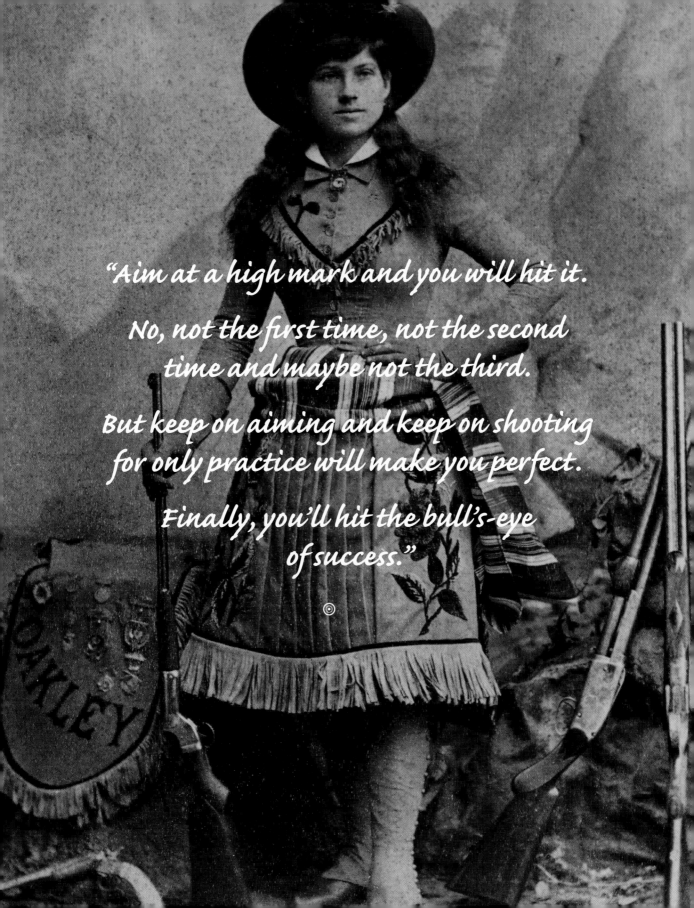

"Aim at a high mark and you will hit it.

No, not the first time, not the second time and maybe not the third.

But keep on aiming and keep on shooting for only practice will make you perfect.

Finally, you'll hit the bull's-eye of success."

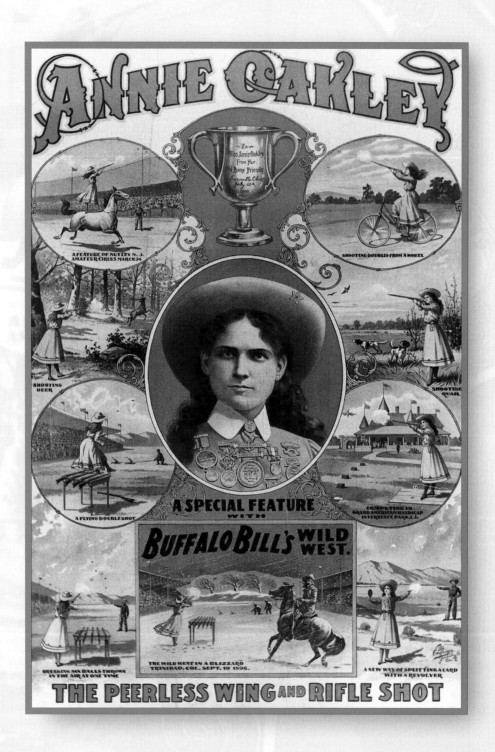

This 1901 poster captured highlights from Annie's career as the world's most celebrated female sharpshooter.

When I was growing up, my Grandpa John often spoke of his sister Annie Oakley. He would recall their happy childhood days in a houseful of girls held together with the faith, love, and strength of their Quaker mother. "Annie was a fussy little girl who tackled everything with precision, from her sewing to her shooting," he would say. "She was pure in heart and spirit. I never heard her utter a cuss word in her life. She prayed on her knees every night."

Imagine his dismay, then, when some popular portrayals of my great-aunt Annie cast her as a coarse and ignorant woman, which she was not. My grandparents and parents were angered and saddened about this perception that Annie Oakley was less than a lady.

With the concerns of our family in mind, my cousin and I chose to form the Annie Oakley Foundation in 1984. Dedicated to setting the record straight, the Foundation has attempted to separate the truth from the stories about Annie that the management of Buffalo Bill's Wild West invented to boost attendance at her shows.

Annie became a larger-than-life legend under the guidance of the Wild West promoters and the tender, watchful care of her lifelong true love, Frank Butler. Yet I doubt that her goal was fame, or even acclaim. At first, she simply was proud that she could use her skill to save her poor family from hunger. To be able to make a living participating in the sport that she loved gave her great satisfaction, and the worldwide honors she achieved allowed her to help people on a grander scale.

In fact, Annie was widely known for her philanthropic work. She helped widows and orphans and deserving young women who wanted to further their educations. These good works reflect her true character and are one of the main reasons she is an excellent role model for young people today.

"Every night, no matter how tired we all were, mother washed our hands and feet, brushed and plaited our hair into pigtails . . . and sang hymns with us and prayed God to watch over us."

◎

Way over in western Ohio, almost as far as you can go without leaving the state, there is a two-lane highway that cuts through fields of corn and soybeans and farms full of fat, healthy pigs. The road runs north and south through Darke County, past Greenville, Ansonia, Rossburg, North Star—small towns with histories as rich as their soil. Tragic Indian wars were fought here, as European settlers hoping to live on the land came up against the Native American inhabitants. In 1795, the chiefs of 13 Indian tribes signed the Treaty of Green Ville, ending the wars and opening up the entire Northwest Territory for settlement.

For decades, this picturesque stretch of road was named after General "Mad Anthony" Wayne, the man who helped bring about the Green Ville treaty. But in the summer of 2000, the state of Ohio renamed the highway as a tribute to one of its distinguished native daughters. The Annie Oakley Memorial Pike is just a stone's throw from where the world's most famous sharpshooter was born, lived as a child, died, and is buried. Although she is remembered as a symbol of the Wild West, Annie's roots were firmly in Ohio.

Annie's parents, Jacob and Susan Wise Moses, came to Darke County from central Pennsylvania, where they had run a small inn. The parents of three daughters, Jacob and Susan were eking out a living at the inn until a careless guest knocked over an oil lamp and burned their wooden building to the ground. Left homeless, Jacob remembered the tales he had heard of western Ohio's fertile

Annie Oakley traveled all over the United States and Europe, but she often returned to Ohio. This portrait was taken in Columbus.

farmland. In the spring of 1855, he and his wife brought their daughters to the small town of Woodland in Darke County, where they cleared some land and built a cabin from the trees they cut down.

Two more daughters were born, although one died before she was a year old. Then, on August 13, 1860, the couple's sixth daughter entered the world. Susan and Jacob named her Phoebe Ann, but her sisters quickly gave her the nickname Annie. As a child, Annie was on the slender side, with thick, dark hair and bright, blue-gray eyes. She loved the outdoors from her earliest days and was intrigued by the mysteries of the woods that surrounded her family's farm. She preferred exploring those woods and helping her father with farm chores to the cooking, cleaning, and canning that her mother did inside. Annie collected brush for the fire, gathered corn from the fields, and helped build fences around the farm. Although the family was still growing—brother John was born in 1862 and sister Hulda in 1864—everyone pitched in. They shared good times and a hope for an even better future.

Then the hard pioneer life took its toll in a sudden and unexpected way. One winter morning in 1866, Annie's father loaded the family's wagon with corn and wheat. Jacob Moses planned to bring these grains to be ground at the local mill, 14 miles away, and then to stop at the general store for coffee, sugar, and rice. As he made his way past woods and farmland, the skies darkened, and it began to snow. Soon the winds picked up, blowing the snow every which way and making travel nearly impossible.

In the Moses cabin, Jacob's family grew more and more anxious as they watched the blinding snow. Day turned into night, and they

OHIO

Darke County
• Springfield
• Dayton
• Cincinnati

Annie Oakley spent both the beginning and end of her life in Darke County, Ohio. The illustration spread across these two pages shows Greenville in 1925, the year before Annie's death.

"Little Sure Shot"

Annie Oakley

★ 1884 ★ BUFFALO BILL CODY'S WILD WEST $1 US SOUVENIR

INDIANA
OHIO

Joseph Shaw home ■ **North Star**

■ Annie's birthplace

■ Woodland (now Willowdell)

Darke County

■ Annie's & Frank's graves

ANNIE OAKLEY MEMORIAL PIKE (U.S. HWY. 127)

Greenville ●

Darke County ■ Infirmary

0   miles   5
0   kilometers   8

↓ To Cincinnati, 70 miles

strained to see or hear any sign of Jacob's wagon. It wasn't until midnight that they heard the crunch of the wagon's wheels on the snow. "Mother threw the door wide open into the face of the howling wind," Annie would write years later. They all rushed out to find Jacob sitting upright in the seat, "with the reins around his neck and wrists, for his dear hands had been frozen so he could not use them. His speech was gone." Jacob Moses had made it home, but he developed pneumonia from his battle with the elements. Several weeks later, he died.

Annie was only five and a half years old when her father passed away, leaving her mother to raise seven children alone. Susan Moses

Farmers helped change the landscape of western Ohio by clearing the land for their crops. In the mid-1800s, though, Ohio farms like this one were still surrounded by forests for hunting.

rented a smaller farm and moved her family there. Besides taking care of the farm chores, Susan earned a bit of money—$1.25 per week—working as a nurse for women who were having babies. She led an exhausting life, but she did her best to keep the family strong and healthy.

As her mother worked to feed her children, Annie, at age seven, took it upon herself to help. Her father had taught her how to make animal traps by digging small trenches, covering them with heavy cornstalks, and filling them with just enough grains of corn to attract the quails, pheasants, and squirrels that roamed the nearby woods. "Each day I found fresh meat for the family larder in my traps," Annie later wrote. The catch was a welcome addition to the family's meager meals, but soon Annie figured out a more effective way to put food on the table.

Annie and her family were Quakers, and like other members of this Protestant sect, they did not believe in fighting wars or engaging in violent behavior. However, the Quakers did allow their members to carry guns as they journeyed west for protection against the unknown challenges of frontier life. Jacob Moses had brought a rifle from Pennsylvania, and Susan kept it over the fireplace in their new home. One day when Annie was eight years old, she climbed up and, with her brother John's help, carefully took it down.

Annie embraced the chance to hunt, even though it was an experience generally reserved for boys. "My mother and sisters thought my prowess with the gun was just a little tomboyish," she later wrote.

Annie wrote that she "stuffed in enough [gun]powder to kill off a buffalo" the first time she used her father's rifle. "What a kick that old gun had," she added. "It flew right back at my nose."

"My mother . . . was perfectly horrified when I began shooting and tried to keep me in school, but I would run away and go quail shooting in the woods or trim my dresses with wreaths of wild flowers."

◎

Annie would tell the story of her first hunt many times, and over the years the details changed. It's unclear now whether she hunted a squirrel or a rabbit, but whatever it was, Annie claimed she brought the animal down with a single shot. She continued to provide fresh game for her family and as a teenager became so skilled that she regularly sold part of her kill to the local grocer. Eventually, Annie would earn enough money with her rifle to pay off the $200 mortgage on her mother's house. "I don't know how I acquired the skill," she once said. "I suppose I was born with it."

Along the way, however, life in the Moses home grew tougher. In 1867, Annie's mother remarried, and a few years later she gave birth to another daughter, Emily. But Annie's stepfather was killed in an accident soon after Emily was born, and her mother found it increasingly difficult to make ends meet. She sent Annie's sister Hulda to live with a neighboring family. Later, when Annie was ten, her mother sent her to live with Samuel and Nancy Ann Edington, who ran the Darke County Infirmary in Greenville.

Annie helped out at the infirmary, in exchange for room and board. She learned to knit, sew, and do fancy embroidery—skills she would use for the rest of her life. But it was a sad place, filled with orphaned children, impoverished adults, and people who were mentally ill. Annie could never forget the faces of the children, in particular. As an adult, she would give generously to charities that were dedicated to helping children.

Not long after Annie arrived at the infirmary, a farmer came looking for a girl to live with his family and help his wife care for their baby son. He promised there would be lots of time to hunt and go to school. Annie volunteered, and after her mother gave her permission, she moved to the man's home, south of Greenville. But Annie quickly learned that the man was a "wolf in sheep's clothing," painting a far from truthful picture of the life she would lead. In fact, he and his wife, whom Annie called the "Wolves," treated her like a slave. On a typical day, she later wrote, "I got up at four o'clock in the morning, got breakfast, milked the cows, fed the calves, the pigs, pumped water for the cattle, fed the chickens, rocked the baby to sleep, weeded the garden, picked wild blackberries, got dinner after digging the potatoes…and picking the vegetables." Only after doing all that could she go hunting and trapping.

If Annie failed to perform any of her duties to the "Wolves" satisfaction, they beat her. One winter night, after she fell asleep while darning socks, the wife shoved the shoeless Annie out the front door and left her in the snow. "I was slowly freezing to death," Annie later wrote. "So I got down on my little knees…and tried to pray. But my lips were frozen stiff and there was no sound." Fortunately, when the woman heard her husband coming home she let Annie back in the house.

Annie put up with this abuse for nearly two years before she ran away and took refuge with the Edingtons at the Darke County Infirmary. When she arrived, she told Nancy how badly she had been treated and showed her the welts and scars that remained on her back from the beatings. The farmer came looking for Annie, but the Edingtons refused to let her return to his home. Instead, they invited the twelve-year-old to stay at the infirmary. Annie lived with the Edingtons for about two years, earning money as a seamstress and learning how to read and write.

When she was 14 or 15, Annie finally went back to live with her family. Her mother was married again, this time to a neighbor, Joseph Shaw, who had bought some land at North Star, north of

Opened in 1856, the Darke County Infirmary housed children and adults together in this three-story brick building. After leaving the "Wolves," Annie stayed in the Edingtons' quarters, separated from the other residents.

Greenville. It was here that Annie began her hunting in earnest. "I glided swiftly through the woods, peeping into each little house for quail and...rabbit," she would write. "I was not what they call a 'game hog.' There was plenty, and I just had to help pay [the mortgage] for the new home." What her family couldn't eat, Annie sent to the grocer in Greenville, who sold it to hotels in Cincinnati, 80 miles away. She wrote, "Each mail day I sent hampers of quail done up in bunches of sixes or twelves."

Martin,

888 Clark Street.
CHICAGO.

Within a year of returning to her mother's home, Annie went to visit her sister Lydia, who had married and moved to the Cincinnati area. While she was there, Annie received an invitation from the owner of a hotel that had bought some of her game. The man wondered if she might be interested in a shooting match with an expert marksman who was appearing in the city. Annie accepted the challenge with great hopes of winning the $50 prize.

According to Annie, the match took place in the fall of 1875 just outside Fairmont, where her sister lived. Her opponent was Frank Butler, a man who made a living by performing trick-shooting exhibitions. Although he was only in his mid-20s, Frank had already led an adventurous life. At 13, he'd sailed to the United States from his native Ireland, paying for his journey by helping out on the ship. Once in New York, Frank had earned money by cleaning out a stable, delivering milk with a horse and buggy, and working for two years on a fishing boat. He'd also trained a dog act in the theater and that had led to his own career as a performer. Along the way, he'd gotten married, had two children, and gotten divorced. Little is known about his relationship with his children.

Frank had no idea who his opponent at the shooting match was to be, and he later said, "I almost dropped dead when a little slim girl in short dresses stepped out to the mark with me." The competition called for Annie and Frank each to attempt to shoot 25 live pigeons as they flew out of traps one at a time. Frank shot first and brought down his bird. Then Annie shot and tied the score at one apiece. The competition continued, with each contestant shooting perfectly until Frank missed his 25th bird. Annie had one more shot. If she made it, the $50 was hers. She took aim at her 25th pigeon and shot it clean. She won the contest, and in the process she also won Frank's heart.

"Right then and there I decided if I could get that girl I would do it," Frank told a reporter years later. He walked Annie and her family to their carriage and gave them free passes to his stage show in Cincinnati. When Annie attended the show, she saw Frank shoot

Shooting tournaments were a popular pastime in the late 1800s. Here, a competitor shoots a clay target—called a "clay pigeon"— launched by the man behind the shooter. In their first meeting, Annie and Frank shot live pigeons.

an apple off the head of his French poodle, George. The dog reportedly took one of the apple pieces in his mouth and laid it at Annie's feet. After that, Annie and Frank used George as a go-between as they explored their feelings for each other. "I just had to send greetings to George, and George sent me back a box of candy," Annie would later write. She gave the poodle credit for helping to bring about her marriage to Frank, which, according to Annie, took place on August 23, 1876.

Information is scarce on Annie's early years with Frank. It's likely that Frank continued to travel and perform on the stage, while Annie stayed behind to help her family. By 1881, Frank had joined the Sells Brothers Circus with a shooting partner named Baughman, but he returned to the theater the following year with a new partner, John

◎

Graham. On May 1, 1882, the team of Butler and Graham was scheduled to appear at Crystal Hall in Springfield, Ohio. When Graham became ill, Frank called on Annie to help out. Later, Annie wrote, "I went on with him to hold the objects as he shot, or [so] he thought. But I rebelled."

That spring evening, Annie insisted on taking every other shot, and the audience went wild after she hit the target on her second try. Frank couldn't help but notice this reaction, and Annie became his new shooting partner. Frank taught Annie many of his trick shots and gradually made her the focus of the act. He knew a star when he saw one. "She outclassed me," he later said. Along the way, his wife chose Annie Oakley as her stage name. There are conflicting stories as to why Annie settled on this name. Some people think she took Oakley from a town in Ohio close to where she first met Frank. (Oakley is now

BUTLER & OAKLEY.

This card advertised Frank and Annie's new shooting partnership. The white poodle is George, the dog that helped cement their relationship.

In a publicity photo, Annie poses next to some of her medals (pinned to the Oakley cloth), guns, and a cup that she won in a shooting competition.

part of Cincinnati.) Others believe it was the name of a man who helped her when she ran away from the "Wolves."

Whatever its origin, the name Oakley stuck, and the team of Butler and Oakley was soon traveling around the Midwest performing in theaters and skating rinks. Frank managed the act, booking stage appearances and rooms in theatrical boardinghouses, arranging for transportation, and taking out ads for the couple's performances. Annie used the skills she had developed at the Darke County Infirmary to design and sew her own costumes.

Having grown up in poverty, Annie spent her money carefully, and if the chance to earn a little extra presented itself, she grabbed it. When she and Frank visited a town to appear onstage at night, Annie often spent her days entering shooting matches for prize money. But in March 1884, Annie's busy schedule almost kept her from an encounter that would be important in building her reputation. She and Frank were in St. Paul, Minnesota, appearing in a huge variety show with singers, acrobats, and other performers. After Annie used her rifle to shoot out candle flames and knock corks from bottles, she received a request for a meeting with the Sioux chief Sitting Bull, who was in the audience.

Annie was tired, so she politely refused to meet the chief. But Sitting Bull, whose army had defeated General George Armstrong Custer's troops at the Battle of Little Bighorn in 1876, would not take no for an answer. He continued sending messages to Annie, and she

Sitting Bull met Annie and Frank in 1884. The next year they would work together in Buffalo Bill's Wild West show.

BUFFALO BILL'S

Wild West

COL. W. F. CODY.

Posters were an important way to
advertise the Wild West show. This one
forms Buffalo Bill's image out of snow-
shoes, a tomahawk, a rifle, horse and
buffalo heads, and several other items.

finally went to visit him. The petite markswoman with the long, dark hair reminded Sitting Bull of his daughter, who had died a number of years before. He felt a kinship with Annie and offered to adopt her. Although no official papers were ever filed, Sitting Bull gave Annie an Indian name, *Watanya Cecila,* or Little Sure Shot. He also gave her the moccasins, made by his beloved daughter, that he had worn in the 1876 battle. Frank made sure that people in the entertainment business heard about the experience with Sitting Bull. He knew that it would help distinguish Butler and Oakley from the many other shooting acts that were cropping up across the country.

Just a month after this encounter, Frank and Annie joined the Sells Brothers Circus. The couple were billed as "the champion rifle shots," but they also played supporting roles in comedy skits. After visiting 187 cities in 1884, they signed new contracts for 1885, but that tour wouldn't begin until April. In the meantime, they were intrigued by a new show that they first saw in New Orleans. Buffalo Bill's Wild West, run by "Buffalo Bill" Cody, was in its second year as "an original American

William F. "Buffalo Bill" Cody earned his nickname in 1867,
when he was hired to supply a dozen buffalo a day to feed the
workers of the Kansas Pacific Railroad, who were laying track
across Kansas. He killed 4,280 buffalo in all.

amusement enterprise," and it included a number of shooting and riding acts. Cody, a former army scout, recognized that people were intrigued by the idea of the Wild West, and he'd put together a traveling show to give them a taste of this vanishing bit of history. Frank and Annie thought their shooting act would be a perfect addition, but unfortunately, the show already featured Captain Adam Bogardus, the country's most famous marksman. When they approached Cody about a job, he turned them down.

Left without work until April, Annie and Frank returned to the theater circuit for the winter. In March they heard that Bogardus had quit Buffalo Bill's Wild West, so they approached Cody again. By now, Frank had decided to work in the background, as Annie's manager. To prove that Annie had the talent to hold her own, he offered to have her perform a trial run of three days at no charge. Cody was skeptical; he didn't think that Annie, who weighed only about 110 pounds, would be able to handle the 10-pound shotguns that Adam Bogardus had left behind. But he agreed to the tryout and invited Frank and Annie to catch up with the show in Louisville, Kentucky.

When Annie and Frank arrived at the Louisville Baseball Park, Cody and his performers were out taking part in their daily parade through the city to announce the evening's performance. Frank suggested that Annie use the time to practice her act. He launched one clay pigeon after another into the air, with Annie firing in quick succession. She hit them with her shotgun held right side up, upside down, in her left hand, and in her right. When she was through, a man who had been standing in a corner watching rushed toward her yelling, "Fine! Wonderful! Have you got some photographs with your gun?" The man was Nate Salsbury, Buffalo Bill's business partner. He hired her on the spot.

Annie and Frank would travel with Buffalo Bill's Wild West off and on for the next 17 years. The show presented an overview of the challenges and triumphs of Western life, and its stars were authentic. Real cowboys rode bucking broncos. Real Indians attacked settlers. Real Pony Express riders streaked across the stage. And then came Little Sure Shot, "adopted" daughter of Chief Sitting Bull. She shot the clay pigeons that Frank sent flying skyward, and then laid down her shotgun, tossed up some glass balls, picked up a rifle, and shot the balls before they fell to the ground. A press agent who joined the Wild West several years later described her performance. "Her entrance was always a very pretty one," wrote the agent, Dexter Fellows. "She never walked. She [skipped] in, bowing, waving, and wafting kisses. Her first few shots brought forth a few screams of fright from the women, but they were soon lost in round after round of applause."

Annie often used glass balls as targets. After her shows, the broken glass that littered the field was plowed under.

Annie fit right in with the Wild West company, playing the dual role of mother and sister to many of the men. Still, it was a grueling life. The performers stayed only one or two days at each stop, and in 1885 they logged thousands of miles, traveling by train throughout the eastern and central United States as well as Canada.

Despite the rugged conditions, Annie's quarters were relatively comfortable. She and Frank shared a good-size tent, which housed two folding chairs, a rug, and chintz curtains. At first they had a hammock for napping, but Cody later gave them two cots with blankets, so they could sleep in the tent overnight. And Annie took baths every morning in a collapsible bathtub, which she set up in a corner of the tent.

Buffalo Bill's Wild West ended its 1885 season with a profit of close to $100,000. After spending the winter with Annie's family, Frank and Annie joined Buffalo Bill for the 1886 season, which

During a trip to New York City in September 1884, Buffalo Bill (on the white horse) paraded his troupe through Union Square to announce their upcoming performances.

included a four-week engagement on Staten Island, in New York. That series of shows was so successful—attracting 360,000 visitors in all—that Cody decided to stay in New York for the winter. He adapted his Western drama so that it worked indoors, and moved everyone to Manhattan for a six-month run at Madison Square Garden. In the new show, Annie continued to display her sharpshooting skills, but she also added some thrilling riding tricks.

On March 31, 1887, the Wild West set sail for England and its most ambitious engagement yet. It was Queen Victoria's Golden Jubilee, her 50th year as queen, and Cody took his whole troupe to appear as part of the American Exhibition in London.

"For me, sitting still is harder than any kind of work."

ANNIE
OAKLEY.

While she was in London, a number of reporters stopped by to interview Annie in her tent, which one called "her temporary canvas home." They found comfortable furniture, "knick-knacks," photographs, even a welcome mat and a white picket fence.

An Indian cast member watches as Annie practices in an empty arena during the Wild West's time in London.

*"I really think I have fired
more shots than anyone else.
I know in one year I used 40,000 shot shells;
also several thousand ball cartridges."*

◎

The company set up camp at Earl's Court, a 23-acre area full of gardens and exhibition halls. They would remain there for six months, living in tents with wooden floors and stoves to chase away the chills that were typical of England's rainy climate.

Royalty from England and other European countries came to see the Wild West, and Annie was one of the biggest attractions. "The loudest applause of the night is reserved for Miss Annie Oakley, because her shooting entertainment is clever, precise, and dramatic," a reviewer wrote in one of London's newspapers. British fans liked Annie because she was talented and elegant, and to their minds, an American original. This last impression was supported by an incident that took place when the Prince and Princess of Wales asked her to visit them in their box

Although she didn't consider herself a "cowgirl," Annie worked hard to perfect her horseback riding skills.

When she joined the Wild West, Lillian Smith claimed that Annie Oakley was "done for," but Lillian stayed with the show for only two years.

after a performance. Although Annie was coached about the British custom of greeting the prince before the princess, she ignored the prince's hand and instead shook hands with his wife first. "It is ladies first in America," she told a reporter. "I guess it amazed them a little, but they didn't mind it and they were very sociable."

When the Wild West packed up to move to Manchester, England, for a winter engagement, Annie and Frank elected not to go. Annie had been earning extra money giving shooting lessons and exhibitions at London gun clubs, and Frank thought it was time for her to break out on her own. The couple had also grown tired of Annie's rivalry with Lillian Smith, a teenage sharpshooter from California whom Cody had added to the show for the 1886 and 1887 seasons. Annie had felt so much pressure to compete with Smith that she had let Buffalo Bill's press agent lop six years off her age in her official biography.

After traveling to Berlin, Germany, to present a private exhibition for Crown Prince Wilhelm, Annie and Frank returned to New York. Annie spent the winter challenging local shooting champions to matches—and usually winning. Then she joined up with Pawnee Bill's Frontier Exhibition, a rival Western show, but left to try her hand at acting on the stage. In early 1889, Annie rejoined Buffalo Bill's Wild West, just in time to sail to Paris with them for a new European tour. Annie's rival, Lillian Smith, was no longer with the company.

By this time, Annie Oakley had built a reputation that made her a celebrity and went a long way toward making her a legend.

Annie became good friends with Johnnie Baker, a marksman who also had joined the Wild West in 1885. Both performed a wide variety of shooting tricks, such as those listed in the program from one of Annie's exhibitions.

PROGRAMME
of
Miss Annie Oakley's
Private Performance
Before The Members and Their Friends
of The Union-Club Berlin
On November 13. 1887
At Charlottenburg Rase Cours.

1. Exhibition of Rifle Shooting.
2. Shooting Clay Pigions for straight.
3. Pulling the trap herself.
4. Standing back to trap, turning and firing.
5. The snap shot hitting the pitgin close the trap.
6. Shooting double or from two traps sprung at sam tirms.
7. Picking gun from ground after trap is sprung.
8. Same shot double.
9. Starding 20 feet from the gun, runing and firing after the trap is sprung.
10. Holding gun with one hand throwing ball herself.
11. Throwing two balls herself, bracking both.
12. Throwing ball backwards, picking up gun, and breaking it.
13. Throwing two balls picking ap gun and breaking im.
14. Breaking two balls throwing in air in four seconds.
15. Breaking threeballs in air at the sam tirms.
16. Breaking five balls in five seconds first with rifle others with shot guns changing guns three times.
17. Shooting ath twelf lif pidgings 25 yards rise 20 bor gun.

Buffalo Bill's
WILD WEST
and Congress of
ROUGH RIDERS
of the World

COL. W. F. CODY Prest.

MR. NATE SALSBURY
V. Prest.

ANNIE OAKLEY

MISS ANNIE OAKLEY
"LITTLE SURE SHOT"

JOHNNIE BAKER
"THE COWBOY KID"

This is just one-quarter of the Wild West troupe that went to London in 1887. Annie is standing in the first row at the far right, and Lillian Smith is seventh from the right in the same row. Buffalo Bill is seated in the foreground, and Nate Salsbury is seated at the far left, wearing a top hat.

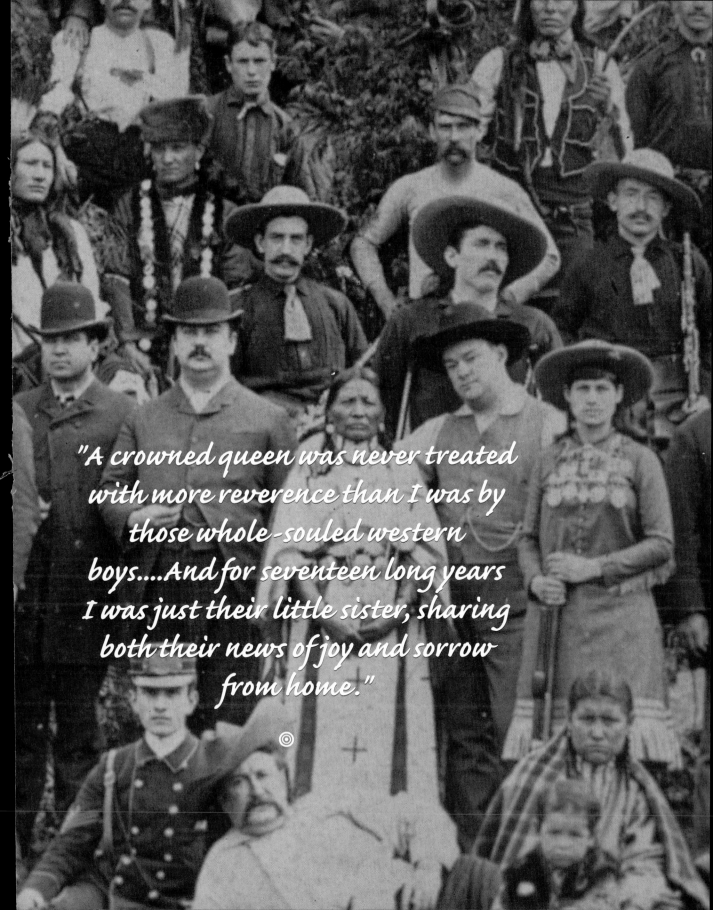

"A crowned queen was never treated with more reverence than I was by those whole-souled western boys....And for seventeen long years I was just their little sister, sharing both their news of joy and sorrow from home."

PRICE THE 3 PENCE

RIFLE QUEEN,

ANNIE OAKLEY.

LIFE,
FEATS,
EXPLOITS,
ADVENTURES
HUNTING

"LITTLE SURE-SHOT."

WONDERFUL
DEAD-SHOT
ON THE
WING
AND RUN.

OF WILD WEST EXHIBITION.

LONDON: THE GENERAL PUBLISHING Cº. 280, STRAND, W.C.

Today, few copies of *The Rifle Queen* survive. This one was owned by Annie's neighbor John D. Donaldson before it made its way to the Nutley Historical Society in New Jersey.

According to some sources, Annie's 1891 Christmas card, mailed to her friends and family from England, was one of the first personalized greeting cards ever sent out at the Christmas season.

LITTLE·SURE·SHOT·

In 1887, a London publisher had come out with *The Rifle Queen*, a 64-page Western novel that claimed to tell the "truthful and stirring story" of Annie's life. The book was pure fiction, with stories of Annie saving a train from robbers, shooting bears and panthers, and bravely killing a wolf that had her arm clasped in its teeth. Still, *The Rifle Queen* helped propel Annie from a skillful sharpshooter to a larger-than-life superhero. The book, as well as the publicity that Buffalo Bill and Frank helped bring about, kept Annie's name in front of the public. People who'd never met her suddenly cared about her and admired her.

That was made abundantly clear late in 1890, when a French newspaper reported that Annie had died. Annie and Frank had spent the previous year and a half in Europe with the Wild West, and at the time of her "death," they were taking a vacation break in England. But the newspaper declared that Annie had died of "congestion of the lungs" in Buenos Aires, Argentina. The news spread quickly through the international press, with the *Cincinnati Commercial*

> *"I am, indeed, very grateful for your many kind words in my obituary. How such a report started I do not know. I am thankful to say I am in the best of health."*

◎

lamenting on January 2, 1891, "Poor Anne Oakley! Dies in a Far-Off Land—The Greatest of Female Shots." Frank and Annie hurriedly sent letters and telegrams to the press assuring everyone that Annie was alive and well. It turned out that an American singer named Annie Oatley had died in Buenos Aires, and a misspelling of her name had caused the confusion.

Buffalo Bill's Wild West continued to tour Europe in 1891 and 1892, adding expert horseback riders from Russia, France, Germany, and other countries to give an international flavor to the show. After extensive engagements in Germany, Belgium, and Holland, Cody and company made their way to the British Isles, finally returning to London for the summer of 1892. By then

POOR ANNE OAKLEY.

The Girl Who Was Barred at Monte Carlo.

Dies in a Far-Off Land—The Greatest of Female Shots.

Jan. 2d

The news of Miss Anne Oakley's death was received in this city with many suspicions of doubt. The shooters of Cincinnati read in The Enquirer cablegrams from Buenos Ayres, South America, of the unfortunate event and are still hesitating what action to take. They can not believe that the vivacious little woman, all nerve and energy, is dead.

She was an honorary member of the Independent Gun Club of this city, the largest gun organization in the State. A prominent Cincinnati sportsman had last week just completed a five-act drama for her, entitled "The Lieutenant of Artillery," and she was to take the part of Lieutenant, the leading character.

The sportsman writes and has quite a reputation as a playwright in the East, under the

NOM DE PLUME OF LEON DEL MONTE.

Though not generally known, Miss Oakley is the wife of Frank Butler, who years ago figured as one of the Austin Brothers, Bachman being his partner. They stood one at each end of the stage and shot peanuts off each other's head, the most dangerous trick in this line of business ever performed. His teachers here were Harvey McMurchy and Al Bandle. She was last here in 1887. She received from the Wild West show $250 per week, her husband acting as her agent.

She was a very saving woman, and purchased for her mother a farm about forty-five miles from Cincinnati. She was

A SMALL WOMAN.

Weighing about 100 pounds; a pronounced brunette, and by the late Indian Sitting Bull was christened "Little Sure Shot," and the name always stuck to her.

The Indians always called her by this name, and when with the show she acted as their banker and kept all their money.

She was barred at Monte Carlo from competing in the great pigeon matches, since from $5 to $10 hinges on every bird sprung

Miss Annie Oakley

Although Annie was skilled with pistols and rifles, she used shotguns in her Wild West performances for safety reasons. The tiny pellets that made up shotgun cartridges traveled only about 60 yards, whereas rifle bullets traveled as far as 1,000 yards. When Annie used a rifle, shopkeepers as far as eight blocks away complained of broken windows.

In one of her most famous shots, Annie spied her target in a mirror and shot it clean without turning around.

EUROPEAN TOUR

Norway
Sweden
British Isles
Glasgow
North Sea
Denmark
Liverpool
Manchester
Netherlands (holland)
Cardiff
London
Belgium
Cologne
Lux.
Berlin
German Empire
Russian Empire
Atlantic Ocean
Paris
Strasbourg
Stuttgart
Prague
ALSACE
Munich
Vienna
France
Switz.
Austro-Hungarian Empire
Venice
Portugal
Spain
Marseille
Italy
Romania
Serbia
Bulgaria
Black Sea
Barcelona
Mont.
Rome
Naples
Ottoman Empire
Mediterranean Sea
Greece
AFRICA

0   200 mi
0   300 km

First half of tour,
April 1889–August 1890

Second half of tour,
April 1891–October 1892

1889—1892

Annie and Frank were shocked at the poverty in many of the European cities they visited, but they were impressed by the beauty of Italian art and architecture.

Annie was a favorite of the British people, loved by royalty and common folks alike, and treated with kid gloves by the press. "Miss Annie Oakley possesses one of the gentlest and kindest dispositions that one could ever wish to own," wrote a reporter after interviewing her that summer. "Her pleasant manner and her soft cheery voice are only excelled by her accuracy of aim and adroitness with the rifle."

Although Annie was thrilled to be in London again, she was anxious for the Wild West's tour to end so she could get back to the United States and see her family. That finally happened in October, when Buffalo Bill's troupe set sail for New York after three and a half years abroad. With six months off until they had to rejoin the show for a long run in Chicago, Annie and Frank decided to settle

After 17 years of marriage, Annie and Frank finally had a home to call their own when they built this house at 304 Grant Avenue in Nutley, New Jersey.

In actual footage from Thomas Edison's 1894 film, Annie rapidly shot at fixed targets and at a series of balls that Frank threw into the air.

down—as much as their nomadic life would allow. They purchased a plot of land in Nutley, New Jersey, and went about designing a three-story house. Just ten miles from New York City, Nutley was home to a number of artists and entertainers. Living there would allow Frank and Annie to pursue their cultural and business interests while still enjoying the peace and quiet of a small town.

Annie and Frank moved into the house in December 1893, and soon their lives began to follow a pattern. They would be on the road with the Wild West from late March through early October and then head back to Nutley to perform exhibitions or pursue other projects. One of these involved Thomas Edison, inventor of the motion picture camera. In the fall of 1894, Annie accompanied Buffalo Bill and some Indians from the show to West Orange, New Jersey, where they were among the first people to be filmed by Edison. Annie's movie, which was only 80 seconds long, showed her firing a rifle 25 times in 27 seconds and then shooting glass balls tossed in the air. After this pioneering performance, Annie went to London, where she appeared in a stage play called *Miss Rora* about an expert sharpshooter and horsewoman, written especially for her.

ANNIE OAKLEY Many Years a Feature with BUFFALO BILL.

IN A STARTLING PICTURE OF THE WILD WEST

THE

WESTERN GIRL

THE GREAT CLIFF SCENE.
NANCE BARRY SAVES LIEUT. HAWLEY.

THE WESTERN VILLAGE STREET.
THE OLD MUSIC HALL.
THE CANYON OF THE COLORADO by MOONLIGHT
PRESENTING
THE GREAT HOLD-UP SCENE
AND THE
TEST OF THE WORLD'S FAMOUS RIFLE SHOT.
THE RESCUE OF THE U. S. SOLDIER.

In the 1902 play, *The Western Girl*, Annie starred as Nance Barry, a Colorado pioneer who fought villains and rescued her loved ones.

As the 19th century drew to a close, Annie took stock of her life. The Wild West had reversed its policy of playing long engagements in one location. Instead, the troupe was traveling all around the United States, logging as many as 11,000 miles per season and performing in 130 towns or more. Although Annie and Frank had their own living quarters on the Wild West's 52-car train, life on the road was starting to take its toll. "I have thought several times I would not go with the show another year," Annie told a reporter in 1899, "but I always do."

That changed after a train wreck abruptly ended the 1901 season. The accident took place at 3:20 a.m. on October 29, as Cody and company were traveling from North Carolina to Virginia in a caravan of three separate trains. The engineer of an oncoming freight train pulled onto a side track to let the first train pass, but he didn't realize there were two more to come. He hit the second train head-on, killing more than 100 horses that were in the first five cars and jolting the passengers to the floor. Annie was thrown from her bed and slammed into a trunk, but sources differ on how badly she was hurt. Some say she received only slight injuries to her hand and back. Others say her back injury was quite serious, requiring several operations to repair. At any rate, Annie was shaken up enough to act on her thoughts of quitting. Soon after the accident, Frank wrote a letter to Buffalo Bill stating that he and Annie felt it was time to leave "the dear old Wild West."

Audiences applauded Annie's heroic deeds onstage as they had in the arena. She received six curtain calls when *The Western Girl* played in Camden, New Jersey, on Christmas Day 1902.

With a brown wig covering her white hair, Annie looked a lot younger than her 51 years when she posed for this photograph in 1911.

Frank accepted a job with the Union Metallic Cartridge Company, which made ammunition for guns, and Annie took part in shooting matches and exhibitions. She also pursued stage work, starring in *The Western Girl,* another show written just for her. But Annie put her acting career on hold when she learned about an article that appeared in two Chicago newspapers on August 11, 1903. That day, the *Chicago Examiner* and the *Chicago American* reported that Annie Oakley was in a Chicago jail after pleading guilty to stealing a man's pants to get money to buy illegal drugs. The story was picked up by newspapers nationwide, and Annie was livid. She wrote to many of the papers to state in no uncertain terms that she had not been in Chicago for months and she had not committed any crime. She demanded that the newspapers print a retraction and said, "Someone will pay for this dreadful mistake."

This souvenir postcard shows a bullet hole shot through the heart on the front and an autograph from Annie on the back.

Annie had worked her whole life to build an excellent reputation and live up to her billing as a role model and a hero. She was not about to let her hard work be ruined by false newspaper reports. Most papers did print retractions, and several investigated further. They found that the woman in jail was actually an actress who had once appeared on stage under the name "Any Oakley."

Although the retractions pleased Annie, they did not satisfy her. She filed lawsuits against 55 newspapers for blackening her good name and spent much of the next seven years testifying in court about the emotional hardship the news articles had caused. In the end, she won or reached out-of-court settlements in 54 of the cases, coming away with more than a quarter million dollars. But more important than the money, which hardly made up for her expenses

When Annie went up in this airplane, she had planned to shoot at targets on the ground. She decided just to pose for pictures, though, after realizing that she might not be able to control her shots and might hurt someone.

and lost income, was the feeling of justice that the verdicts brought. In 1910, Frank told the publication *Forest and Stream,* "I want to say right here, that when she entered these suits, it was not money but vindication she was after."

With the lawsuits finally behind her, Annie went back to work. In 1911, she joined the Young Buffalo Wild West, a show much like Buffalo Bill's. Although Annie now wore a brown wig—her hair had turned white soon after the train accident—she still wowed audiences with her sharpshooting and her rope tricks. But after three more seasons on the road, 53-year-old Annie decided to call it quits. She and Frank had sold the New Jersey house in 1904, and now they built a cottage on the water near Cambridge, Maryland. They would spend summers there, hunting and fishing with their new dog, Dave. When the weather grew colder, they'd head south for prolonged stays at hotels in Leesburg, Florida, or Pinehurst, North Carolina.

Although they had retired from the Wild West circuit, Annie and Frank continued to perform exhibitions and give shooting lessons at local gun clubs. Annie was particularly interested in teaching women to shoot, both for sport and for protection. "I think every woman should learn the use of firearms," she had written as far back as 1907. In Pinehurst, she spent two hours every morning giving free shooting lessons to women. Over the years, she estimated that she taught 15,000 women to shoot.

When the United States entered World War I in 1917, Annie wrote to the U.S. secretary of war offering to train a women's

Annie tested shells from the Union Metallic Cartridge
Company in an open field and offered women tips on
gun safety in a 1904 newspaper pictorial.

division to defend the home front. "I can guarantee
a regiment of women for home protection," she wrote, "every
one of whom can and will shoot if necessary." She received no
response to her offer, but she and Frank found other ways to help
the war effort. Besides giving shooting exhibitions at U.S. Army
posts, they trained Dave to retrieve money that people wrapped in
handkerchiefs and then hid. (He smelled the handkerchiefs before
they were hidden.) One day Dave tracked down $1,625 in hidden
money. Everything he retrieved was given to the Red Cross, earning
him the nickname "Dave, the Red Cross Dog."

As friends and family looked on, a group of women took a shooting lesson from Annie (at the railing, second from right) in March 1918 near Pinehurst, North Carolina.

"*I would like to see every woman know how to handle [firearms] as naturally as they know how to handle babies.*"

Following the end of the war in 1918, Annie continued to donate her time and money to causes that concerned her. Two of her sisters had died of tuberculosis, and Annie honored their memories by visiting hospital patients suffering from the disease and giving exhibitions to raise money for their care. She also donated money to orphanages and helped as many as 20 young women pay for their college educations.

As the 1920s began, Annie considered bringing her talents to the newest form of show business sweeping the nation, motion pictures. But her plans ended in a tragic accident on November 9, 1922. Annie and Frank were traveling to Leesburg, Florida, in a chauffeur-driven Cadillac when the driver was forced onto the shoulder by a passing car. As he tried to get back on the road, the car overturned. Although Frank escaped unharmed, Annie was pinned underneath. She suffered a fractured hip and a shattered right ankle and spent the next six weeks in a hospital. Frank rented a room in a building across from the hospital, and he and Dave visited her every day.

Annie was flooded with close to 2,000 letters and telegrams from friends and fans, and she left the hospital determined to get back on her feet. Although she would have to wear a brace on her right

By 1921, Dave was popular enough to have his own personalized Christmas card.

Annie, Dave, and Frank posed for a family portrait in 1921.

leg for the rest of her life, by the end of February she was able to spend a good portion of the day out of bed. But just as she was starting to feel like herself again, another tragedy struck. While Frank and Dave were out for a walk, the dog spotted a squirrel and sprinted after it. He ran into the street as a car was approaching and was hit—and killed instantly. The news of Dave's death was carried in newspapers and magazines nationwide. *American Field* remembered Dave's war work and called him "one who did his bit to give true democracy to the world."

After Dave's death, Annie and Frank slowly returned to a limited schedule of exhibitions and travel. They were spending a great deal of time visiting Annie's family in Ohio, and in 1925 they rented a house in Dayton. Annie started to write her memoirs, but failing

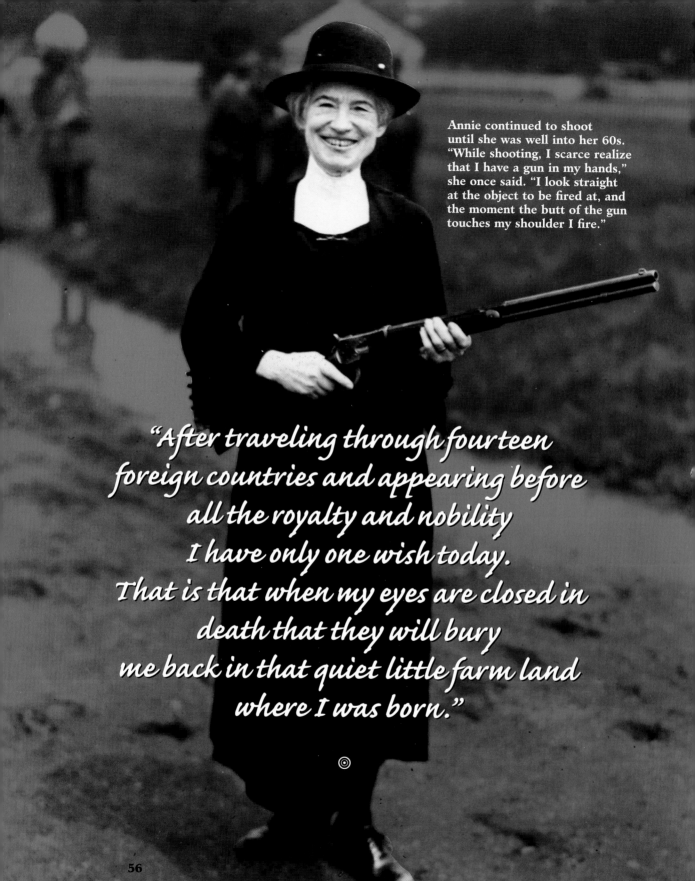

Annie continued to shoot until she was well into her 60s. "While shooting, I scarce realize that I have a gun in my hands," she once said. "I look straight at the object to be fired at, and the moment the butt of the gun touches my shoulder I fire."

"After traveling through fourteen foreign countries and appearing before all the royalty and nobility I have only one wish today. That is that when my eyes are closed in death that they will bury me back in that quiet little farm land where I was born."

health was catching up with both her and Frank. Annie had been diagnosed with pernicious anemia, a blood disorder, and she was weak and tired. Frank's throat was giving him trouble, and he suffered other ailments as well.

As the summer of 1926 drew to a close, Annie urged Frank to go ahead with his plans to return to North Carolina for the winter, even though she didn't feel up to the journey. He agreed, but first he headed to Royal Oak, near Detroit, where he planned to ask Annie's niece to go south with him. When Frank arrived, though, Annie's niece felt that he was not strong enough to make the trip south. Instead, she fixed up a room for him in her home. Meanwhile, in Ohio, Annie realized that she needed full-time nursing care and moved to a boarding-house in Greenville. Soon afterward, she contacted the local funeral parlor to discuss her funeral arrangements. She told the director that she had no strength left and knew the end was near.

Annie died on November 3, 1926. She was 66 years old. Frank died in Royal Oak 18 days later at age 76.

Today, small signs direct visitors to Annie's grave in Brock Cemetery (above), the site of her family's home in North Star (below), and other landmarks near the Annie Oakley Pike.

Following Annie's wishes, her body was cremated, and her ashes were put into a trophy cup she had won in her shooting days. The trophy, which was placed in a solid oak box, was kept in a vault at the funeral home. After Frank's funeral, his body and Annie's ashes were buried side by side in Brock Cemetery, just off the highway in western Ohio that's now called the Annie Oakley Memorial Pike.

When *Annie Get Your Gun* returned to Broadway in 1999, it won Tony awards for Best Musical Revival and Best Actress in a Musical (Bernadette Peters).

A nnie Oakley was both a symbol of an age gone by and a trailblazer whose achievements opened up new opportunities for women. As a sharpshooter with Buffalo Bill's Wild West, she helped people relive the perilous and heroic days of the frontier, when Indians defended their land against people heading west to find their fortunes. As one of the few women in Buffalo Bill's troupe, she became a role model for females young and old. Annie showed them that they could succeed in a job usually done by men, and she encouraged them to learn to protect themselves and to embrace the adventures that awaited them in the great outdoors.

Irving Berlin's memorable songs helped make *Annie Get Your Gun* a hit. Sheet music, like the piece above, was reissued when the film version was released.

Annie was the first female Wild West superstar, and one of the first American women whose achievements brought her worldwide fame. Her legend started to grow while she was still with Buffalo Bill, and it continued to grow after her death. In 1935, actress Barbara Stanwyck portrayed her in *Annie Oakley,* a feature film that told a fictionalized version of her relationship with Frank. Eleven years later, *Annie Get Your Gun* put Annie's story to music. This musical, a smash hit, ran for three years on Broadway and is revived often on stages all over the world. It came

Although it distorted the truth about Annie's life, *Annie Get Your Gun*, with original star Ethel Merman, introduced the sharpshooter to a whole new generation of fans.

E GREATEST RIFLESHOT
IN THE WORLD

out in movie form in 1950. From 1954 through 1957, TV audiences got to visit with Annie Oakley every week in the half-hour *Annie Oakley* series. The series inspired novels, comic books, board games, and clothing for girls who wanted to dress like their TV hero.

In these shows and movies, the Annie Oakley who is presented is a far cry from the real woman. If the details of Annie's life got in the way of the story the writers wanted to tell, they changed them, giving her blond hair instead of brown, having her live on a ranch in Texas, or making her lose in her first shooting match with Frank. That, no doubt, would have upset the real Annie, who fought so hard to protect her reputation. But although the details are important, it's Annie's character that should be remembered: The inner strength that helped her survive a tough childhood, her determination to succeed, her integrity, her loyalty, her kindness. Annie Oakley steered her own course through life at the turn of the century, and in the process she helped change people's ideas of just how extraordinary a woman could be. As her friend, humorist and newspaper columnist Will Rogers, put it, "Annie Oakley's name, her lovable traits, her thoughtful consideration of others will live as a mark for any woman to shoot at."

As TV's *Annie Oakley,* actress Gail Davis pledged to wear her blond hair in pigtails for all public appearances. Her image graced the cover of novels (top) and comic books (bottom and left).

CHRONOLOGY

August 13, 1860	Phoebe Ann (Annie) Moses is born in Woodland, Ohio
1866	Father dies from pneumonia
1868	Shoots a gun for the first time
1870–1872	Lives with and works for the "Wolves"
1875	Meets Frank Butler and beats him in a shooting match
August 23, 1876*	Marries Frank Butler
1884	Tours with Sells Brothers Circus as Frank's shooting partner
1885	Joins Buffalo Bill's Wild West
1887	Goes to England with Buffalo Bill's troupe
1889–1892	Tours Europe with the Wild West
December 29, 1890	French newspaper reports that she died in Buenos Aires
1892	Builds a home in Nutley, New Jersey
1894	Thomas Edison films her shooting
October 29, 1901	Injured in a train wreck in North Carolina; quits Buffalo Bill's show

*Note: An 1881 marriage certificate contradicts the 1876 date Annie gave in her writings.

1902	Appears onstage in *The Western Girl*
1903	Newspapers erroneously report that she was arrested in Chicago
1904–1910	Goes to court against 55 newspapers that ran the false report
August 18, 1908	Mother dies
1913	Buys a home in Cambridge, Maryland; Dave, an English setter, joins the family
1915–1922	Teaches women to shoot at Pinehurst, North Carolina
1918	Tours Army camps with Frank and Dave
November 9, 1922	Seriously hurt in a car accident near Leesburg, Florida
February 25, 1923	Dave is hit by a car and dies
November 3, 1926	Dies from pernicious anemia, a blood disorder, in Greenville, Ohio.**
November 21, 1926	Frank Butler dies from "senility" in Detroit, Michigan.

**Note: Some people believe she actually died of lead poisoning, from lead shot.

In 1919 Annie watched as a student shot at flying targets in Pinehurst, North Carolina.

AUTHOR'S NOTE: GETTING THE DETAILS RIGHT

Anyone who writes about Annie Oakley comes up against the fact that there are conflicting accounts of many of the details of her life. For example, although it is generally accepted that Annie was born in 1860, some sources give the year of her birth as 1866. This can be traced to the promoters of Buffalo Bill's Wild West show, who thought Annie would seem even more extraordinary if she were six years younger.

Other discrepancies developed the same way. Annie was a public figure for much of her life, and she allowed her husband, Frank, and the Wild West promoters to create an image for her that sometimes embellished or changed the truth. So there are two accounts of Annie's first meeting with Frank, conflicting versions of when they were married, and reports of amazing feats that Annie never performed, such as shooting a cigarette out of the mouth of Germany's Kaiser Wilhelm. (Apparently, she didn't do that, but it does seem that she shot one out of his hand.)

When conflicting accounts exist, I have consulted a number of different sources and then chosen the alternative that seems most reasonable. For example, in her unfinished autobiography, written in the 1920s, Annie said her first meeting with Frank took place outside Cincinnati, Ohio. Although Frank later wrote that it took place about a hundred miles away, near Greenville, I have used Annie's version of the event.

There are also several spellings of Annie's original last name, possibly due to a lack of formal education among some of her family members. Many researchers believe her parents used the name Moses, but Annie called herself Mozee for a number of years. Bess Edwards, Annie's grandniece, believes the name was Mozee, but her grandfather, Annie's brother John, used Moses. So have I.

Despite the uncertainties surrounding some of the details, there's no doubt that Annie Oakley was an inspiration to many people during and after her lifetime.

RESOURCES

Quotes from Annie Oakley are taken from her unfinished, unpublished 1926 biography, *The Story of My Life,* and her interviews in contemporary newspapers and magazines.

Books

Kasper, Shirl. *Annie Oakley.* Norman, Oklahoma: University of Oklahoma Press, 1992.

A thorough, well-written biography from a journalist who admired Annie growing up.

Riley, Glenda. *The Life and Legacy of Annie Oakley.* Norman, Oklahoma: University of Oklahoma Press, 1994.

A scholarly assessment of Annie's life.

Sayers, Isabel S. *Annie Oakley and Buffalo Bill's Wild West.* New York: Dover Publications, Inc., 1981.

An inviting survey that's full of photographs and illustrations.

Scrapbooks

Buffalo Bill Historical Center

720 Sheridan Avenue
Cody, Wyoming 82414
Phone: 307-587-4771

Annie kept four huge scrapbooks that have just about every article published about her during her lifetime. The originals are here, but copies have been loaned out to other libraries and museums.

Video

"Annie Oakley: Crack Shot in Petticoats," *Biography,* A&E Television Networks, 1998.

An entertaining and mostly accurate installment from the *Biography* TV series.

Web Sites

Annie Oakley Foundation

P.O. Box 127
Greenville, Ohio 45331
Phone: 937-547-3966
www.annieoakley.org

Does research and educational programs about Annie. Also produces a newsletter.

Dorchester County Public Library

http://www.dorchesterlibrary.org/library/aoakley.html

Features an excellent article on Annie from a library near her cottage in Maryland.

Places to Visit

Garst Museum

205 North Broadway
Greenville, Ohio 45331
Phone: 937-548-5250

Has a room packed with artifacts from Annie's life.

National Women's Hall of Fame

76 Fall Street
Seneca Falls, New York 13148
Phone: 315-568-8060

Annie was inducted into the Hall in 1993.

PICTURE CREDITS

Abbreviations used: Annie Oakley Foundation: AOF; Buffalo Bill Historical Center, Cody, Wyoming: BBHC; Circus World Museum, Baraboo, Wisconsin: CWM; Denver (Colorado) Public Library Western History Collection: DPL; Garst Museum, Greenville, Ohio: GM; Library of Congress: LOC; Nutley (New Jersey) Historical Society: NHS.

Front cover DPL #F22055; Back cover Circus World Museum; pp. 2-3 BBHC #MS94; p. 5 Culver Pictures; p. 6 CWM; pp. 6-7 CWM; p. 9 DPL #F24607; p. 10 GM; pp. 10-11 Collection of Sue Macy; p. 12 Culver Pictures; p. 13 Culver Pictures; p. 14 AOF; p. 17 Ohio Historical Society; p. 18 GM; p. 20 Culver Pictures; p. 21 AOF; p. 22 GM; p. 23 LOC LC-USZ62-109538; p. 24 LOC LC-USZ62-53793; p. 25 LOC LC-USZ62-2051; p. 26 (left) CWM; p. 26 (right) DPL, Collection of Nate Salsbury #NS-664; p. 28 AOF; p. 29 DPL, Collection of Nate Salsbury #NS-251; pp. 30-31 AOF; p. 32 DPL, Collection of Nate Salsbury #NS-455; p. 33 DPL # F27156; p. 34 BBHC #P.69.1588; p. 35 (left) Chris Gimmeson, BBHC #MS6-Series VII; p. 35 (right) CWM; pp. 36-37 AOF; p. 38 NHS; p. 39 GM; p. 40 Chris Gimmeson, BBHC #MS6-Series VII; pp. 40-41 BBHC MS6.57.S CPBK; p. 41 DPL, Collection of Noah H. Rose #X-22137; p. 42 BBHC, Vincent Mercaldo Collection #P.71.356; p. 44 NHS; p. 45 Archival film and video materials from the collections of the LOC; p. 46 AOF; p. 47 BBHC #P.69.71; p. 48 CWM; p. 49 NHS; p. 50 AOF; p. 51 (upper) CWM; p. 51 (lower) BBHC #MS6.S7.SCPBK; pp. 52-53 © Bettmann/CORBIS #U72951INP; p. 54 BBHC #MS6.S7.SCRBK; p. 55 GM; p. 56 LOC; p. 57 (upper) AOF; p. 57 (lower) Sue Macy; p. 58 (left) Courtesy of the Estate of Irving Berlin; p. 58 (right) Courtesy of the Producers of *Annie Get Your Gun;* p. 59 Culver Pictures; p. 60 (all) Courtesy of Terrie Davis; p. 61 UPI/CORBIS-Bettmann #U84342INP

ACKNOWLEDGMENTS

The author expresses her appreciation to the following people for sharing their resources, photographs, and expertise: Judy Logan of the Garst Museum in Greenville, Ohio; Maja Keech of the Library of Congress Prints and Photographs Division; Ann Marie Donoghue of the Buffalo Bill Historical Center in Cody, Wyoming; Erin Foley of the Circus World Museum in Baraboo, Wisconsin; Timothy Feleppa of Culver Pictures, Inc.; Lori Swingle of the Western History/Genealogy Department of the Denver (Colorado) Public Library; Ed Stecewicz and Richard O'Connor of the Nutley (New Jersey) Historical Society; and Bill Dayne of the Newark (New Jersey) Public Library. Also, special thanks to Bess Edwards of the Annie Oakley Foundation for her guided tour of Greenville and her dedication to telling the true story of her great aunt Annie's life.

INDEX

EDUCATIONAL EXTENSIONS

1. How did Annie Oakley's determination help her to succeed in a male-dominated world? How does the author use evidence to demonstrate this?

2. What lessons did you learn from reading about the life of Annie Oakley? Use primary and secondary sources to determine key events and concepts from Annie's life.

3. Discuss the meaning behind this famous Annie Oakley quote: "Aim at a high mark and you will hit it. No, not the first time, not the second time and maybe not the third. But keep on shooting for only practice will make you perfect. Finally, you'll hit the bull's-eye of success."

4. Discuss ways in which determination can help you complete difficult tasks in your own life. Cite examples from the text to support your claims.

MORE TO PONDER...

- What does it mean to be successful?
- Describe the success of a person you've read about.
- How does reading about others' accomplishments inspire you?
- Research a topic from the book. Compare and contrast information and details that you found from different sources.
- How do people change the world?
- How can you make a lasting impact on society?